piano · vocal · guitar

# CLASSIC JAZZ STANDARDS

ISBN 0-7935-8317-9

**HAL•LEONARD® CORPORATION**
7777 W. BLUEMOUND RD. P.O. BOX 13819 MILWAUKEE, WI 53213

For all works contained herein:
Unauthorized copying, arranging, adapting, recording or public performance is an infringement of copyright.
Infringers are liable under the law.

Visit Hal Leonard Online at
www.halleonard.com

# CLASSIC JAZZ

| | | | |
|---|---|---|---|
| 4 | **ALICE IN WONDERLAND**<br>Isham Jones | 64 | **FLAMINGO**<br>Duke Ellington |
| 7 | **ALL THE THINGS YOU ARE**<br>Ella Fitzgerald | 70 | **GIRL TALK**<br>Neal Hefti |
| 10 | **ANGEL EYES**<br>Frank Sinatra | 67 | **THE GLORY OF LOVE**<br>Count Basie |
| 13 | **THE BIRTH OF THE BLUES**<br>Frank Sinatra | 74 | **GOOD MORNING HEARTACHE**<br>Billie Holiday |
| 18 | **THE BLUE ROOM**<br>Bix Beiderbecke | 77 | **HOW DEEP IS THE OCEAN**<br>Coleman Hawkins |
| 23 | **CARAVAN**<br>Duke Ellington | 80 | **I GET ALONG WITHOUT YOU VERY WELL (EXCEPT SOMETIMES)**<br>Red Norvo |
| 28 | **CHEROKEE**<br>Charlie Barnet | 88 | **I MEAN YOU**<br>Thelonious Monk |
| 31 | **COME SUNDAY**<br>Duke Ellington | 85 | **I SHOULD CARE**<br>Gerald Wilson |
| 34 | **COMES LOVE**<br>Benny Goodman | 90 | **I'LL BE AROUND**<br>Mills Brothers |
| 39 | **DANCING ON THE CEILING**<br>Ella Fitzgerald | 98 | **I'LL REMEMBER APRIL**<br>Charlie Parker |
| 44 | **DON'T BLAME ME**<br>Charlie Parker/Miles Davis | 102 | **I'M GLAD THERE IS YOU**<br>Sarah Vaughan |
| 48 | **DON'T GET AROUND MUCH ANYMORE**<br>Ella Fitzgerald | 93 | **I'VE GOT THE WORLD ON A STRING**<br>Frank Sinatra |
| 52 | **EASY TO LOVE**<br>Ella Fitzgerald | 108 | **IF I WERE A BELL**<br>Miles Davis |
| 54 | **EV'RY TIME WE SAY GOODBYE**<br>Benny Goodman Quintet;<br>Vocal by Peggy Mann | 111 | **IN THE WEE SMALL HOURS OF THE MORNING**<br>Frank Sinatra |
| 58 | **A FINE ROMANCE**<br>Count Basie | 114 | **IT MIGHT AS WELL BE SPRING**<br>Ella Fitzgerald |

*These standards have been recorded by many artists. We have selected a particularly memorable recorded performance by a prominent artist for each song.*

# STANDARDS

| | | | |
|---|---|---|---|
| 118 | LITTLE GIRL BLUE<br>**Les Brown** | 167 | SPRING WILL BE A LITTLE LATE THIS YEAR<br>**Carmen McRae** |
| 120 | LOLLIPOPS AND ROSES<br>**Jack Jones** | 170 | SQUEEZE ME<br>**Louis Armstrong** |
| 122 | LONG AGO (AND FAR AWAY)<br>**Art Pepper** | 173 | A SUNDAY KIND OF LOVE<br>**Claude Thornhill** |
| 125 | MIDNIGHT SUN<br>**Lionel Hampton** | 176 | TAKE FIVE<br>**Dave Brubeck** |
| 132 | ON A SLOW BOAT TO CHINA<br>**Phil Woods** | 182 | TANGERINE<br>**Jimmy Dorsey with Helen O'Connell & Bob Eberly** |
| 135 | OUT OF NOWHERE<br>**Lena Horne** | 186 | TENDERLY<br>**Rosemary Clooney** |
| 140 | PERDIDO<br>**Duke Ellington** | 188 | THERE IS NO GREATER LOVE<br>**Billie Holiday** |
| 143 | POLKA DOTS AND MOONBEAMS<br>**Bud Powell** | 192 | THEY SAY IT'S WONDERFUL<br>**Frank Sinatra** |
| 146 | ROCKIN' CHAIR<br>**Louis Armstrong** | 196 | THE THINGS WE DID LAST SUMMER<br>**Frank Sinatra** |
| 150 | SATIN DOLL<br>**Duke Ellington** | 198 | WHAT A DIFF'RENCE A DAY MADE<br>**Dinah Washington** |
| 153 | SKYLARK<br>**Frank Sinatra** | 201 | WHAT'S NEW?<br>**Maynard Ferguson** |
| 156 | SMALL FRY<br>**Bing Crosby and Johnny Mercer** | 204 | YOU BROUGHT A NEW KIND OF LOVE TO ME<br>**June Christy** |
| 160 | SOMEBODY LOVES ME<br>**Lena Horne** | | |
| 164 | SONG FOR MY FATHER<br>**Horace Silver** | | |

# ANGEL EYES

Words by EARL BRENT
Music by MATT DENNIS

Moderately Slow

Try to think that love's not a-round, still it's un-com-fort-'bly near.

My old heart ain't gain-in' no ground be-cause my An-gel Eyes ain't here.

An-gel Eyes that old dev-il sent,

Copyright © 1946 (Renewed 1973) by Music Sales Corporation (ASCAP)
International Copyright Secured   All Rights Reserved
Reprinted by Permission

# THE BIRTH OF THE BLUES
### from GEORGE WHITE'S SCANDALS OF 1924

Words by B.G. DeSYLVA and LEW BROWN
Music by RAY HENDERSON

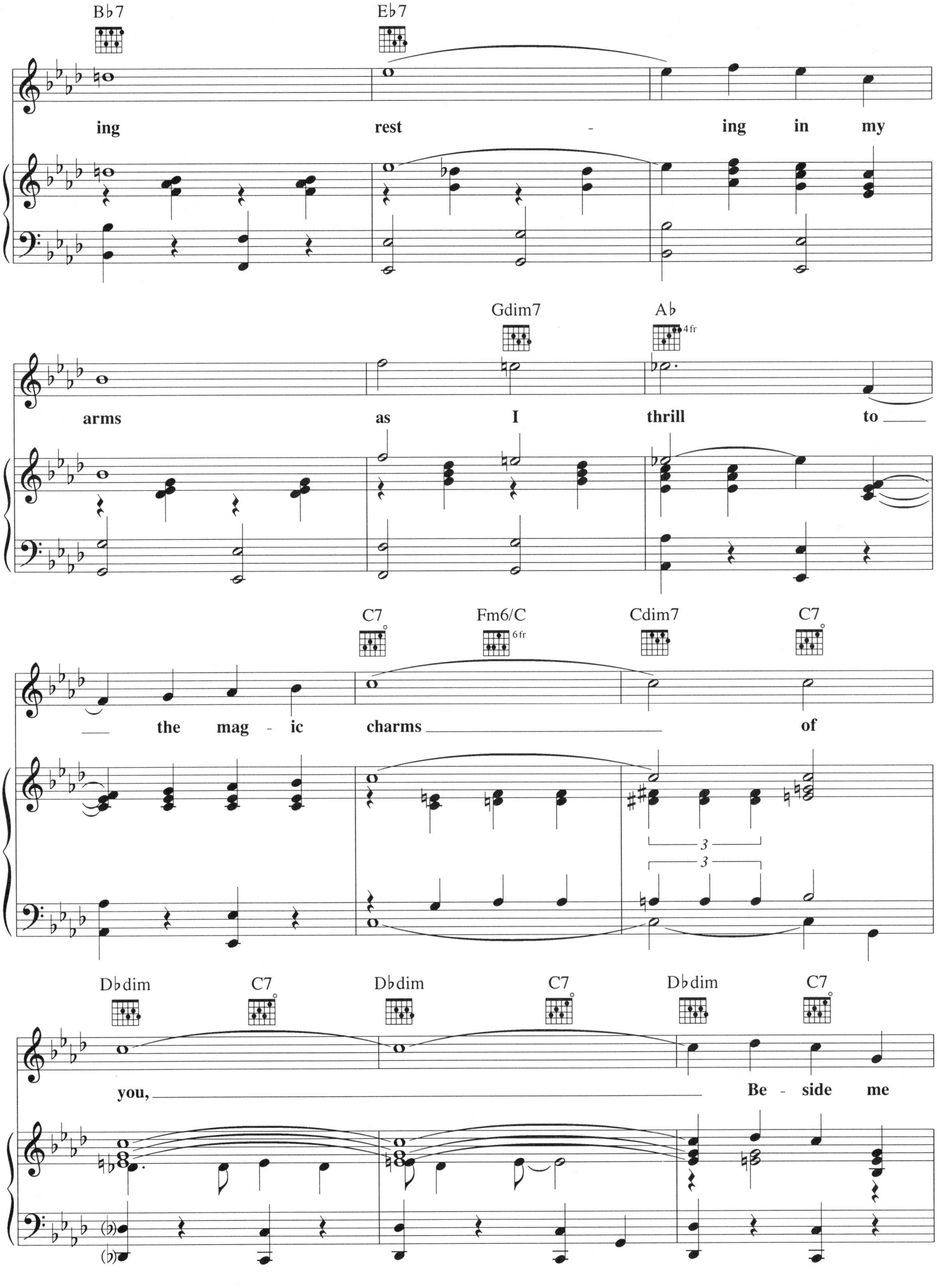
B♭7
E♭7
ing rest - ing in my
Gdim7
A♭
4fr
arms as I thrill to
C7
Fm6/C
6fr
Cdim7
C7
the mag - ic charms of
3
3
D♭dim
C7
D♭dim
C7
D♭dim
C7
you, Be - side me

# CHEROKEE
(Indian Love Song)

Words and Music by
RAY NOBLE

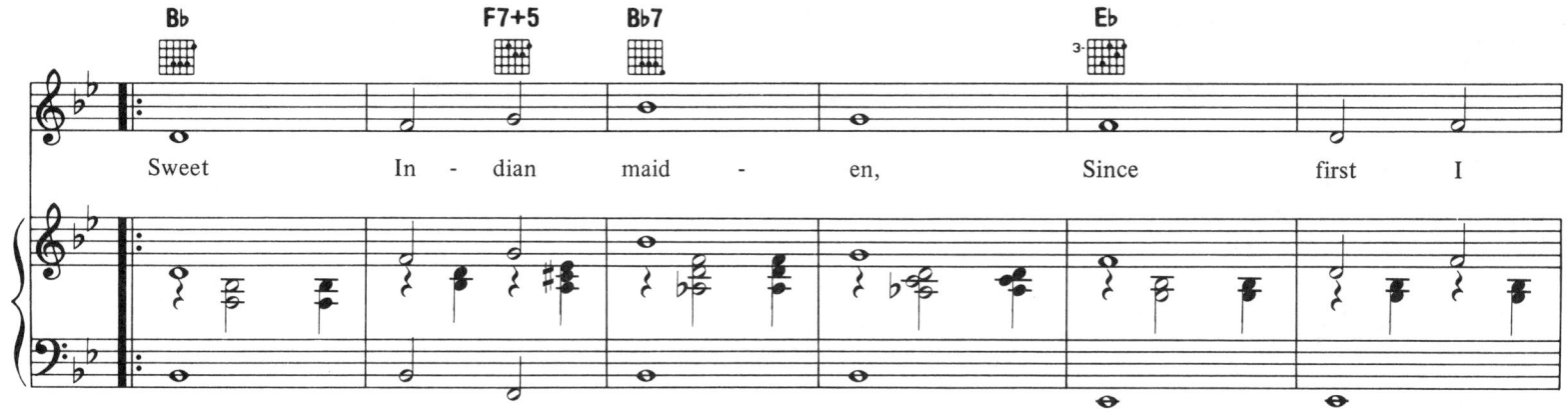
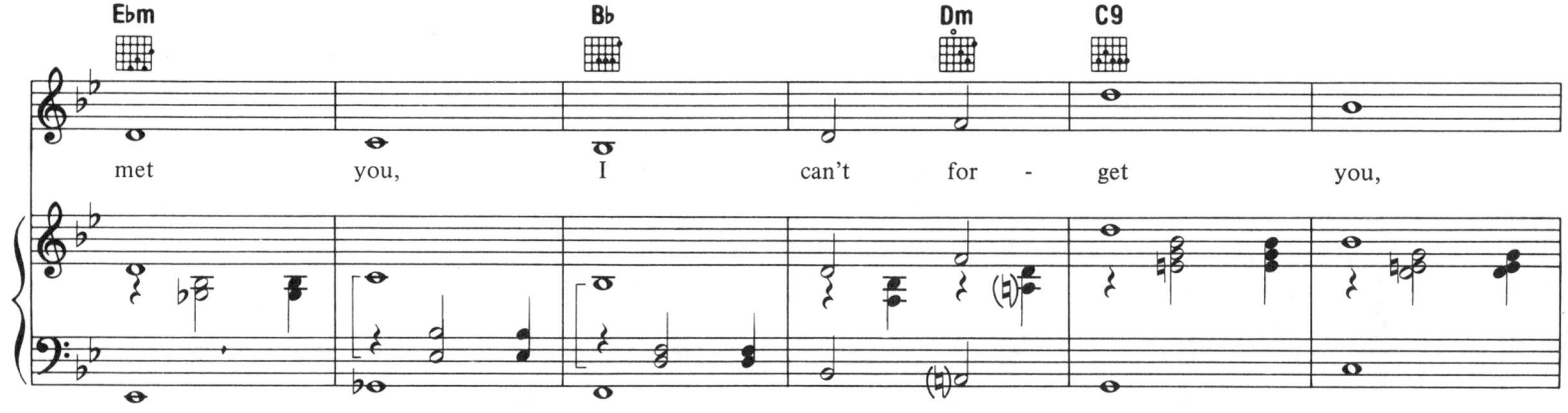
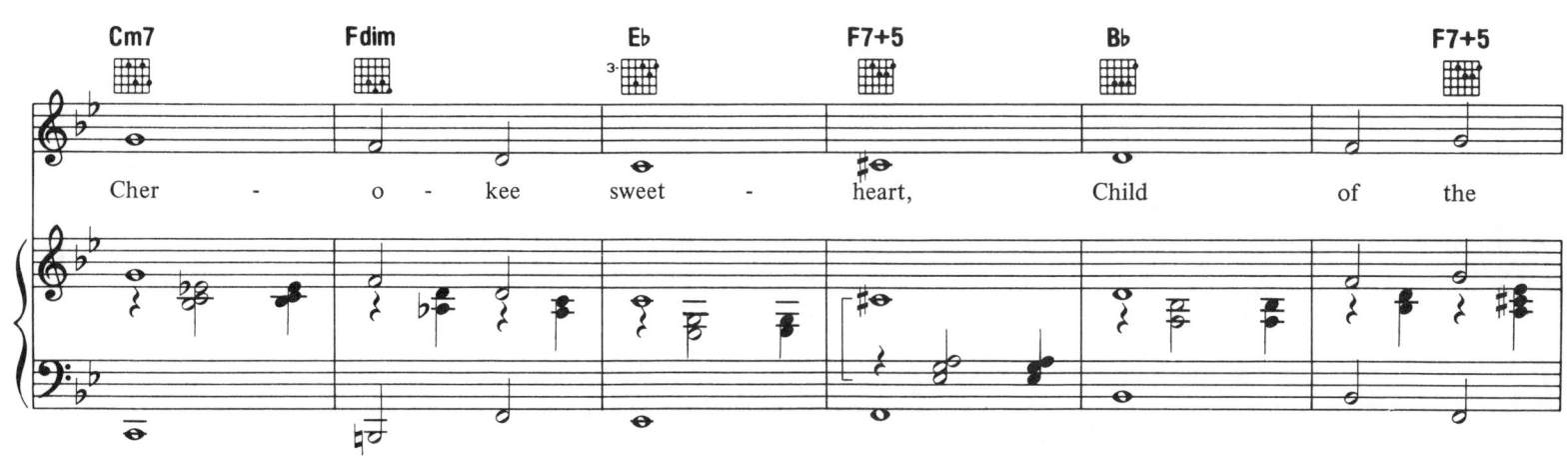

Copyright © 1938 The Peter Maurice Music Co., Ltd., London, England
Copyright Renewed and Assigned to Shapiro, Bernstein & Co., Inc., New York for U.S.A. and Canada
International Copyright Secured   All Rights Reserved
Used by Permission

# A FINE ROMANCE
## from SWING TIME

Words by DOROTHY FIELDS
Music by JEROME KERN

# FLAMINGO

Lyric by ED ANDERSON
Music by TED GROUYA

# GIRL TALK
## from the Paramount Picture HARLOW

Words by BOBBY TROUP
Music by NEAL HEFTI

# I SHOULD CARE

Words and Music by SAMMY CAHN,
AXEL STORDAHL and PAUL WESTON

# I MEAN YOU

By THELONIOUS MONK
and COLEMAN HAWKINS

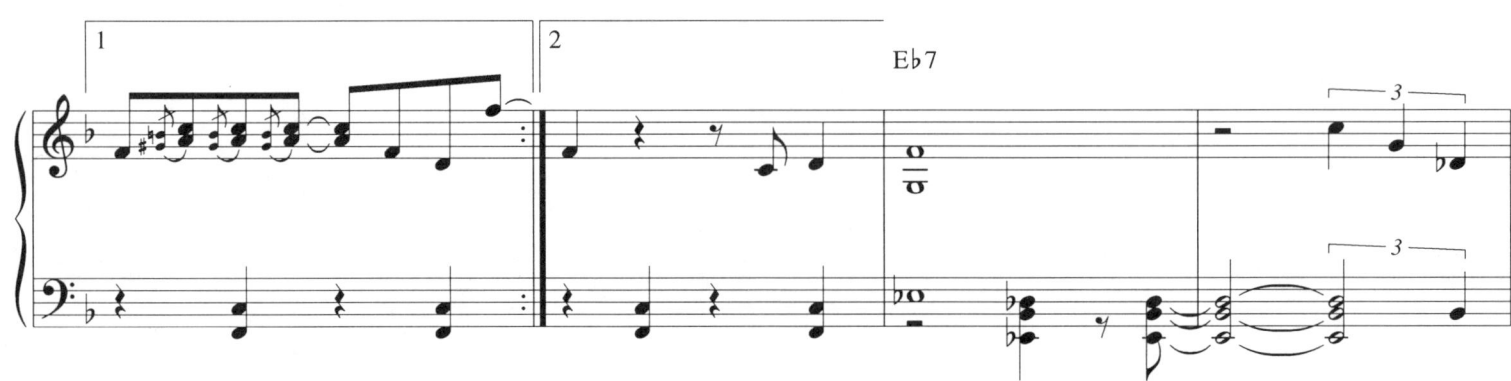

Copyright © 1947 (Renewed) by Music Sales Corporation (ASCAP)
International Copyright Secured   All Rights Reserved

# I'VE GOT THE WORLD ON A STRING

Lyric by TED KOEHLER
Music by HAROLD ARLEN

# I'M GLAD THERE IS YOU
(In This World of Ordinary People)

Words and Music by PAUL MADEIRA
and JIMMY DORSEY

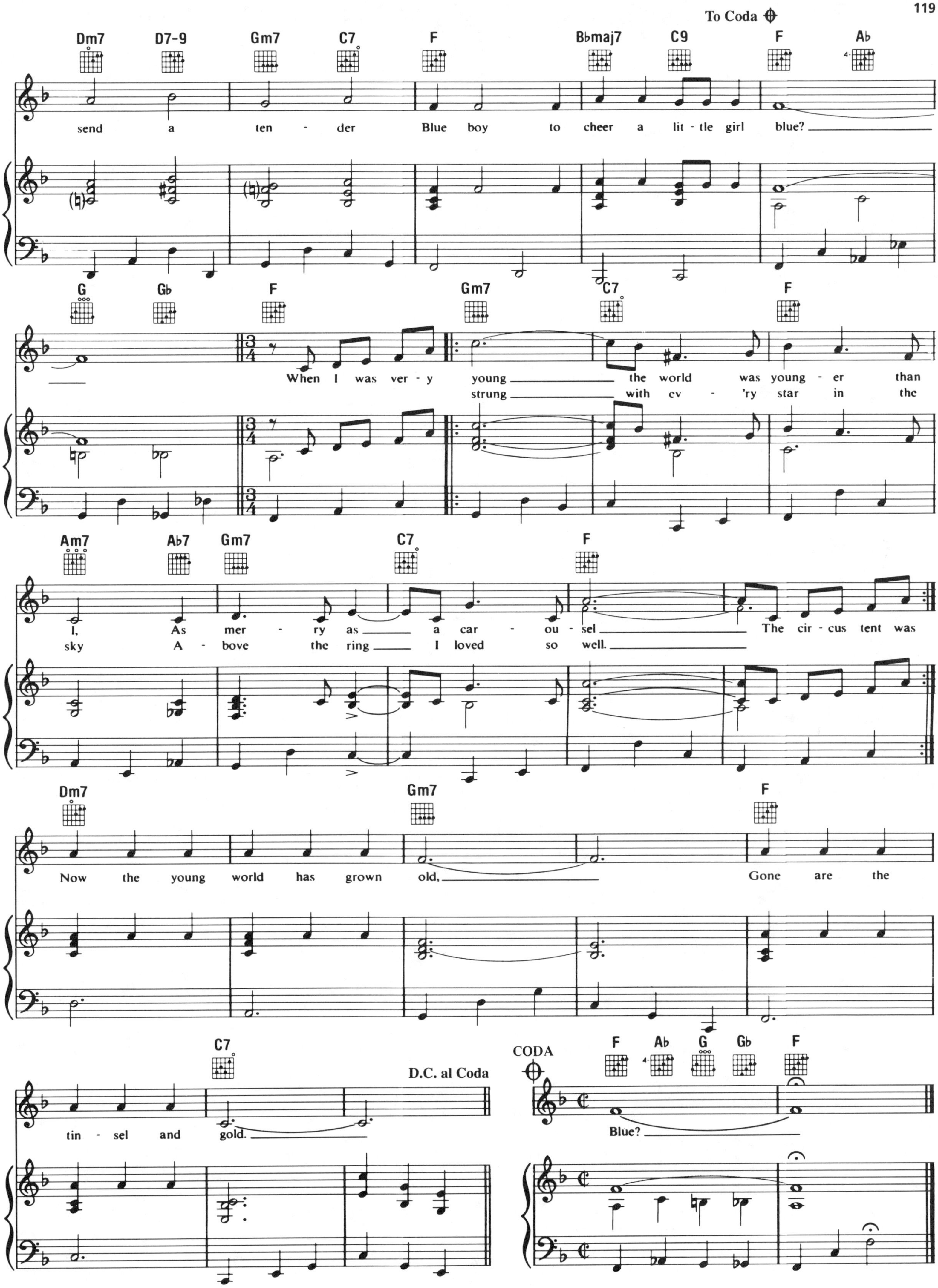
To Coda
Dm7 D7-9 Gm7 C7 F Bbmaj7 C9 F Ab
send a ten - der Blue boy to cheer a lit - tle girl blue?
G Gb F Gm7 C7 F
When I was ver - y young the world was young - er than
strung with ev - 'ry star in the
Am7 Ab7 Gm7 C7 F
I, As mer - ry as a car - ou - sel The cir - cus tent was
sky A - bove the ring I loved so well.
Dm7 Gm7 F
Now the young world has grown old, Gone are the
C7
tin - sel and gold.
D.C. al Coda
CODA
F Ab G Gb F
Blue?

# MIDNIGHT SUN

Words and Music by LIONEL HAMPTON,
SONNY BURKE and JOHNNY MERCER

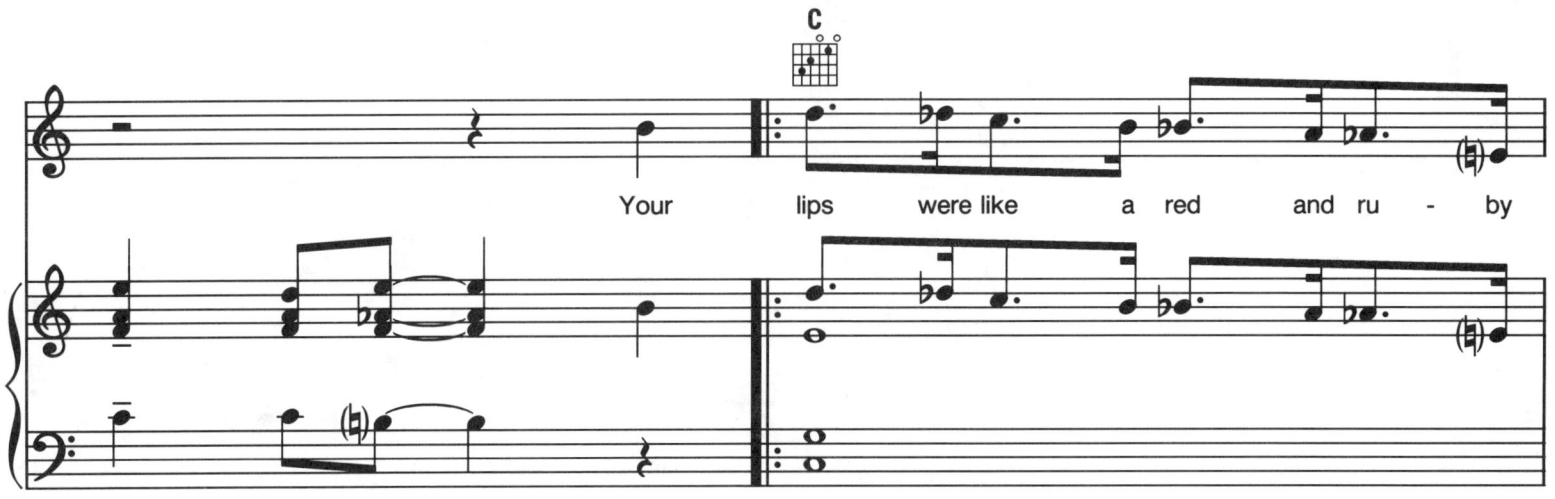

Your lips were like a red and ru-by

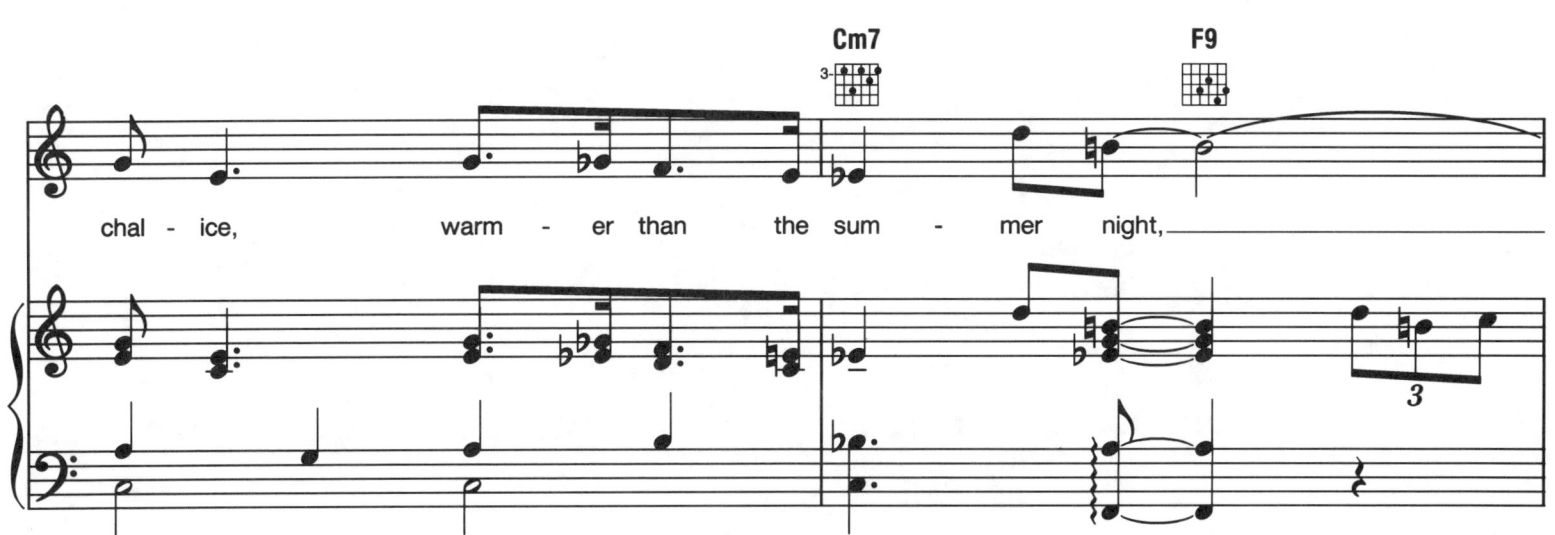

chal-ice, warm-er than the sum-mer night,

Copyright © 1947 (Renewed) by Regent Music Corp. and Crystal Music Publishing, Inc.
International Copyright Secured  All Rights Reserved

# ON A SLOW BOAT TO CHINA

By FRANK LOESSER

# POLKA DOTS AND MOONBEAMS

Words by JOHNNY BURKE
Music by JIMMY VAN HEUSEN

# ROCKIN' CHAIR

Words and Music by
HOAGY CARMICHAEL

# SATIN DOLL
from SOPHISTICATED LADIES

Words by JOHNNY MERCER and BILLY STRAYHORN
Music by DUKE ELLINGTON

Medium Swing

*Use pedal sparingly*

Cig-a-rette hold-er which wigs me o-ver her shoul-der, she digs me Out cat-tin' that sat-in doll.

Copyright © 1958 (Renewed 1986) and Assigned to Famous Music Corporation, WB Music Corp. and Tempo Music, Inc. c/o Music Sales Corporation in the U.S.A.
Rights for the world outside the U.S.A. Controlled by Tempo Music, Inc. c/o Music Sales Corporation
International Copyright Secured  All Rights Reserved

# Song for My Father

Words and Music by
HORACE SILVER

Moderate Bossa Nova

# Spring Will Be A Little Late This Year

from the Motion Picture CHRISTMAS HOLIDAY

By FRANK LOESSER

© 1943 (Renewed) FRANK MUSIC CORP.
All Rights Reserved

# A SUNDAY KIND OF LOVE

173

Words and Music by BARBARA BELLE, LOUIS PRIMA,
ANITA LEONARD and STAN RHODES

© Copyright 1946 by MCA MUSIC PUBLISHING, A Division of UNIVERSAL STUDIOS, INC.
Copyright Renewed
International Copyright Secured  All Rights Reserved
MCA music publishing

# TAKE FIVE

By PAUL DESMOND

Moderately fast ♩=176

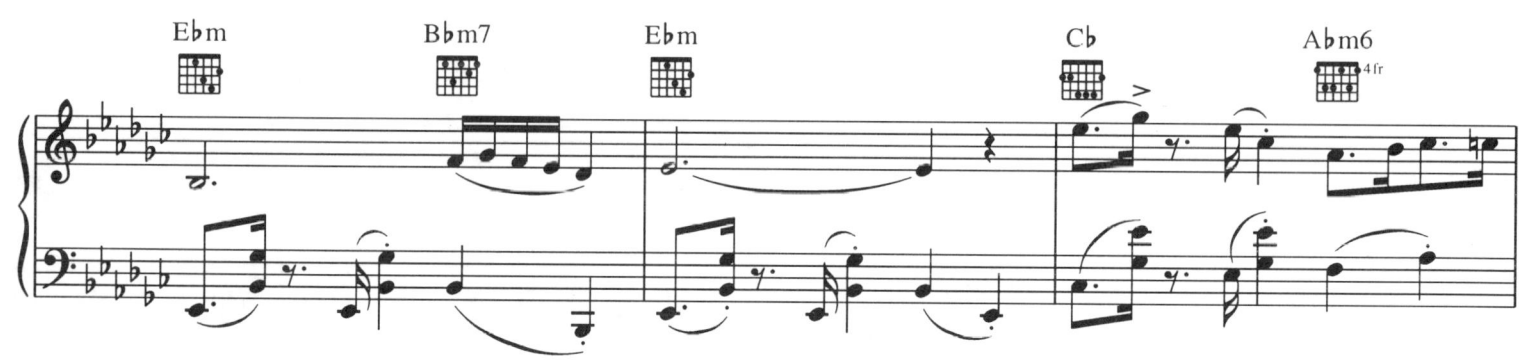

© 1960 (Renewed 1988) Desmond Music Company
All Rights outside the USA Controlled by Derry Music Company
International Copyright Secured   All Rights Reserved

# THEY SAY IT'S WONDERFUL
from the Stage Production ANNIE GET YOUR GUN

Words and Music by
IRVING BERLIN

# WHAT A DIFF'RENCE A DAY MADE

English Words by STANLEY ADAMS
Music and Spanish Words by MARIA GREVER

Copyright © 1934 by Edward B. Marks Music Company
Copyright Renewed and Assigned to Stanley Adams Music, Inc. and Zomba Golden Sands Inc.
All Rights for Stanley Adams Music, Inc. Administered by The Songwriters Guild Of America
International Copyright Secured   All Rights Reserved
Used by Permission

# Jazz Folios from Hal Leonard

### 20 Ragtime Jazz Classics For Piano
20 classics, arranged as piano solos, including: Maple Leaf Rag • Chromatic Rag • The Entertainer • Evergreen Rag • Champagne Rag • and more!

00490247 Piano Solo ................... $9.95

### The Big Book Of Jazz
75 of the world's greatest jazz classics, including: Autumn Leaves • Bewitched • Birdland • Cherokee • A Fine Romance • Flying Home • Have You Met Miss Jones • Honeysuckle Rose • How High The Moon • (I Can Recall) Spain • I've Got You Under My Skin • Jelly Roll Blues • Lullaby Of Birdland • Morning Dance • A Night In Tunisia • A Nightingale Sang In Berkeley Square • Route 66 • Take The "A" Train • and more.
00311557 Piano/Vocal/Guitar ........... $19.95

### Cabaret Songbook
54 essential songs for any current or aspiring cabaret singer. This collection includes: Ain't Misbehavin' • Another Op'nin' Another Show • Down In The Depths • Everything's Coming Up Roses • How High The Moon • I'll Be Seeing You • I've Got You Under My Skin • Let Me Entertain You • My Way • One • People • Piano Man • and more. 232 pages.
00490488 Piano/Vocal/Guitar ........... $15.95

### The Definitive Jazz Collection
A once-in-a-lifetime collection of 90 of the greatest jazz songs ever compiled into one volume. Includes: Ain't Misbehavin' • All The Things You Are • Birdland • Body And Soul • A Foggy Day • Girl From Ipanema • Here's That Rainy Day • The Lady Is A Tramp • Love For Sale • Mercy, Mercy, Mercy • Midnight Sun • Moonlight In Vermont • Night And Day • Skylark • Stormy Weather • Sweet Georgia Brown • and more.
00359571 Piano/Vocal/Guitar ........... $24.95

### Jazz Ballads
Over 40 sentimental favorites, including: Autumn In New York • Bewitched • Body And Soul • Misty • Mood Indigo • Moonlight In Vermont • My Funny Valentine • A Nightingale Sang In Berkeley Square • Stormy Weather • When I Fall In Love • and more.
00311672 Piano/Vocal/Guitar ........... $14.95

### Jazz, Blues, Boogie & Swing For Piano
A collection of the original sheet music for 48 songs from the era, featuring the arrangements of "Fats" Waller, Art Tatum, Duke Ellington, James P. Johnson, Albert Ammons, Pete Johnson, Count Basie, Clarence Williams, Jay McShann, Billy Kyle, Zez Confrey.
00129210 Piano Solo ................... $14.95

### Jazz Classics
37 classics, including: Body And Soul • My Funny Valentine • Stella By Starlight • The Very Thought Of You • When I Fall In Love • and more.

00110027 Easy Piano ................... $14.95

### Jazz Favorites
15 songs, including: April In Paris • Body And Soul • Have You Met Miss Jones? • My Favorite Things • A Night In Tunisia • Sophisticated Lady • and more.

00292054 Piano Solo ................... $12.95

### The Ultimate Jazz Fake Book

Finally! The jazz collection that everyone's been waiting for!

*The Ultimate Jazz Fake Book* includes:
- More than 625 songs important to every jazz library.
- Carefully chosen chords with some common practice chord substitutions.
- Lyrics to accommodate vocalists.
- Easy-to-read music typography.
- Composer and performer indexes.

The selection of songs in *The Ultimate Jazz Fake Book* is a result of an exhaustive effort to represent the many styles of music that make up that beloved idiom we call jazz. The styles found in this collection include: traditional, swing, bebop, Latin/bossa nova, hard bop/modern jazz and Tin Pan Alley standards/show tunes.

*More than 625 songs including:*
All Of Me • And All That Jazz • Birdland • C.C. Rider • Cry Me A River • Deed I Do • Don't Get Around Much Anymore • Maple Leaf Rag • Basin Street Blues • Air Mail Special • Tuxedo Junction • Take The "A" Train • Donna Lee • A Night In Tunisia • Ornithology • Lullaby Of Birdland • Desafinado • Little Boat • The Girl From Ipanema • Solar • Song For My Father • 'Round Midnight • Waltz For Debby • Bag's Groove • I Concentrate On You • I Can't Get Started • Love Walked In • All The Things You Are • A Foggy Day • many, many more!

Spanning more than nine decades of music, *The Ultimate Jazz Fake Book* fills a void for many musicians whose active repertories could not possibly include this vast collection of classic jazz compositions and durable songs.

Available in three editions:
00240079 C Edition .................... $39.95
00240081 Eb Edition ................... $39.95
00240080 Bb Edition ................... $39.95

FOR MORE INFORMATION, SEE YOUR LOCAL MUSIC DEALER, OR WRITE TO:

HAL•LEONARD® CORPORATION
7777 W. BLUEMOUND RD. P.O. BOX 13819 MILWAUKEE, WI 53213

Prices, contents, and availability subject to change without notice. Some products may not be available outside the U.S.A.